LIVING WITH
DOWN'S SYNDROME

Jenny Bryan

HODDER
Wayland

an imprint of Hodder Children's Books

Titles in the series

Living with Asthma	Living with Diabetes
Living with Blindness	Living with Down's Syndrome
Living with Cerebral Palsy	Living with Epilepsy
Living with Deafness	Living with Leukaemia

Series editor: Carron Brown
Book editor: Liz Harman
Cover design: Steve Wheele Design
Inside design: Peter Laws
Consultant: Nick Tapp, Deputy Chief Executive, East Sussex Disability Association

First published in Great Britain in 1998 by
Wayland (Publishers) Ltd

Reprinted in 2000 by Hodder Wayland,
an imprint of Hodder Children's Books

Hodder Children's Books
a division of Hodder Headline
338 Euston Road
London NW1 3BH

© Hodder Wayland 1998

British Library Cataloguing in Publication Data
    Bryan, Jenny
    Living with Down's syndrome
    1. Down syndrome – Juvenile literature
    2. Down syndrome – Patients – Juvenile literature
    I. Title II. Down's syndrome
    362.1'96858842

ISBN 0 7502 2839 3

Printed and bound in Italy by G. Canale and C.S.p.A.

Acknowledgements
The publishers would like to thank Fordwater School, West Sussex, for their assistance
with the photographs on pages 12 and 13, and West Sussex County Council Library
Service for their assistance with the photographs on pages 16 and 17.

Picture acknowledgements
Wayland Publishers Ltd would like to thank: Chapel Studios 26; The Down's
Syndrome Association *cover* (centre), 9 (bottom), 22, 23, 24 (both); Angela Hampton,
Family Life Picture Library *cover* (top left), *cover* (bottom right), 5, 7 (both), 18;
Impact 25; Sally Lewis-Smith 29; The Riding for the Disabled Association 28;
L. Willatt, East Anglian Regional Genetics Service/Science Photo Library 6 (both),
Hattie Young/Science Photo Library 8, 9.

All the other photographs were taken for Wayland by Angela Hampton.
Most of the people who are photographed in this book are models.

The Down's Syndrome Association was consulted in the production of this book.

Contents

Meet Stacey, Richie, Maria and Jack

Stacey has Down's syndrome. Every morning, she and her older sister, Jo, walk to their school, down the road from where they live. Stacey needs extra help with her reading and writing, but not with her favourite lesson, art. She often draws pictures of the family pets, especially their dog, Sammy.

▽ After school, Megan often takes Richie to the playground or to the local swimming pool.

△ Stacey loves playing with Sammy and taking him out for long walks.

Richie is five years old and he has Down's syndrome too. He loves playing with his big sister, Megan. When Mum and Dad first brought Richie home from the hospital, they were very worried about him, but Megan thought the new baby was great. Now, none of them can imagine life without Richie.

◁ Maria and her flatmates enjoy a cup of tea and a chat at the end of the day.

Maria is 22 years old and she shares a flat with three other young women – Sandy, Tina and Rachel. They all have learning difficulties, Sandy is deaf and Maria has Down's syndrome. The four flatmates do their own shopping and look after themselves, with a little help from Liz and Jim who live next door. Maria has a job at the local library.

Jack catches a bus each morning to take him to a special school for children with learning difficulties. The school is in another town, and the journey takes about an hour. Jack likes the other children at the school, but they don't live near him so he can only see them at school. He wishes he could go to the same school as his brother, Ben, so that he could make friends who live nearer his home.

△ Jack's reading has got much better and he often reads to his brother, Ben.

What is Down's syndrome?

If you have Down's syndrome, you have an extra chromosome in each of your cells. Chromosomes carry all the information we inherit from our parents, which affects how we look, grow and feel.

Humans usually have 23 pairs of chromosomes, but people with Down's syndrome have an extra copy of one chromosome. It doesn't sound like much of a difference. But that extra chromosome affects how the body and mind develop. That's why people like Stacey, Richie, Maria and Jack may take longer than other children to learn to walk, speak, read and write.

▽ The chromosomes on the right are those of a person with Down's syndrome, showing three chromosomes in the twenty-first set.

▽ Babies with Down's syndrome need a lot of care and attention, just like other babies.

At birth, babies with Down's syndrome tend to be small and their muscles may be weak. People with Down's syndrome are also more likely to have heart defects, and many have problems with their eyesight or hearing. They also tend to have skin problems and may have a lot of coughs and colds, so they need to take extra care of themselves.

One in every 1,000 babies is born with Down's syndrome. It happens all over the world. Women of all ages can have babies with Down's syndrome, but it is more likely if a woman has a baby when she is in her late thirties or forties.

▷ Toddlers learn quickly, especially if they have plenty of attention and help.

Treatment for Down's syndrome

▽ This baby is being taught to roll across the floor as he reaches for his toys.

Doctors cannot take away the extra chromosome that people with Down's syndrome have. But they can treat many of the health problems that may occur.

Children can have operations to correct heart problems. Wearing glasses or hearing aids can help to improve their eyesight and hearing. They may also need to do special exercises to make their muscles stronger, or have help to improve how they speak.

As they get older, people with Down's syndrome tend to put on weight easily. They have to be careful not to eat too much and to take plenty of exercise to stay fit and healthy. Since people with Down's syndrome may have a lot of coughs and colds, they sometimes need medicine to help them get better.

△ This boy has poor hearing so his mother is teaching him to use sign language to talk to her.

◁ Everyone needs skills to find a job. This man trained to use computers, which helped him get a job.

Like Stacey and Jack, children with Down's syndrome may need extra help with their lessons at school. Adults like Maria can get support and advice about finding jobs and their own places to live. They may also need someone to help them with things like shopping and cooking, and to make sure they are taking proper care of themselves.

Stacey's day

◁ In maths classes, Miss Jackson is on hand to help Stacey with difficult work.

▽ Art is one of Stacey's favourite subjects at school.

Stacey goes to the same lessons as other children at her school. But she and a boy in her class get a little extra help from Miss Jackson, the teacher's assistant. Miss Jackson sits with them during some lessons, such as maths and science, and explains things they find hard to understand. Then they do the schoolwork just like the rest of the class.

In art, drama and PE lessons, Stacey joins in with the other children and doesn't need Miss Jackson's help. Stacey has a part in the school play and she's helping to paint the scenery, too.

Stacey likes some sports more than others. She doesn't like ball games. She tries very hard but she keeps dropping the ball. Some of the children laugh at her and they don't want her in their team. This makes Stacey feel sad.

Stacey is learning to swim

'I really enjoy our swimming lessons at school. I like being in the water, and my friends and I usually end up splashing each other!'

◁ Mum makes sure Stacey does her homework and helps out if Stacey gets stuck.

When she gets home from school, Stacey does her homework. Sometimes she bribes her sister with chocolate so that she will help her. Like her friends, Stacey would prefer to listen to her CDs than do homework, but her Mum can be very strict about homework!

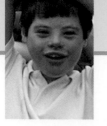

Jack's day

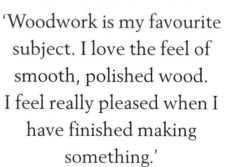

◁ Jack answers lots of questions in class.

J ack goes to a special school where all the pupils have learning difficulties. Some have Down's syndrome, like Jack.

The lessons at Jack's school are the same as at other schools, but the teachers explain things more slowly, so that all the children understand. Jack finds maths rather difficult but he enjoys history and geography.

Jack's special talent

'Woodwork is my favourite subject. I love the feel of smooth, polished wood. I feel really pleased when I have finished making something.'

◁ Jack's teacher is showing him how to use a saw safely.

▽ At break times, Jack and his friends rush outside for a game of football.

Jack also likes woodwork classes. Last term, he made a spice rack for his Mum. At home, Jack's Grandad makes lots of things in his workshop and Jack loves to help. When he grows up, Jack wants to make furniture.

Like Stacey, Jack isn't very good at ball games, but nor are most of the other children in his class, so no one cares and they all have fun. People don't laugh at Jack when he drops the ball, and he doesn't feel left out.

Jack feels tired after the long bus ride home from school. He doesn't know the other children in his street. They all go to the local school and seem to have their own friends, so Jack feels a bit lonely. He usually watches TV in the evening with Ben and their Mum, but sometimes Mum takes Ben and Jack for a bike ride or to the cinema.

Richie faces the bullies

Richie and Megan often take their dog, Bonny, for a walk in the park near their home. One day, they were throwing a ball for Bonny when some boys came over and started laughing at Richie.

'You look funny, your face is all flat,' they said to Richie.

'Thicko, thicko!' they jeered. One of the boys gave Richie a shove and his glasses fell off.

▽ Richie, Megan and Bonny were having a great time until the bullies came along and spoiled it.

'Leave us alone,' shouted Megan. But the boys grabbed the ball and ran off.

Megan was very upset. She hates it when people are unkind to Richie. But Richie said it didn't matter. He picked up his glasses and put them on. He began to make funny faces at Megan and soon they were both laughing.

'Now, you really do look funny,' said Megan, and they started to throw sticks for Bonny to fetch.

Richie doesn't care!

'I don't get upset when people are nasty to me. I wouldn't want to be friends with them anyway!'

▷ Richie soon forgot the bullies and cheered up Megan.

Maria's day

Maria found it hard to get a job. Most people did not want to give her work when they saw she had Down's syndrome. They thought she couldn't do the job. She applied for jobs in shops and at a cinema, but she didn't get them. She kept trying until she got a job at the library. Maria enjoys earning her own money to spend how she likes.

At the library, there is a trolley full of books which people have read and brought back. Maria puts the books back on the shelves. There are many sections in the library, and Maria has to check each book to see where it belongs. Every book has a number on it and Maria has to put the books in the right order on the shelves.

◁ At the library, they gave Maria the chance to prove she could do the job, and she showed them that she could.

Sometimes Maria looks at the books before she puts them back. Once, when she was in the children's section of the library, a little girl asked Maria about the book she was reading. Maria started to tell her all about it, and the little girl liked the story. Her mother listened too, and then she asked Maria about some other books. Now, Maria often helps the children to choose books.

▽ When you're looking for a good book, it helps to get advice from someone who has read them.

Maria loves her job

'I enjoy helping people to choose books from the library because I love reading myself. There are so many books to choose from.'

Growing up

How old were you when your parents first let you go somewhere without them? Maybe it was just a walk to the shops or to cycle or catch a bus to school. Or perhaps you started going to a friend's house to play or do your homework.

No one wants their parents around all the time when they are growing up, and parents like to spend some time on their own, too.

As you grow up, you'll spend more and more time doing what you want to do. You'll choose where to go and what to do, instead of leaving it to your parents or other adults to decide. Sometimes you'll have a good time, sometimes you won't. But at least you can decide for yourself.

◁ Children with Down's syndrome have hobbies, just like everyone else.

▷ These girls love singing along to their favourite bands.

When you leave school, you may go away to college or decide to live with some friends. It's an exciting time because you'll be in charge of your life. If you want to stay in bed all day, you can. If you want to stay up late watching TV, no one will tell you off.

▽ It is good to have a friend to talk to.

If you have learning difficulties, you will also want to make your own decisions. You will want to be as independent as possible. With a little help, you can live like other adults. Like Maria, you may be able to live where there are people who will help out if there is a problem, but do not interfere.

Maria's outing

Maria wanted to go to the cinema, but she needed someone to tell her how to get there. If you were giving her instructions, you would need to explain things very clearly. She isn't deaf, so you wouldn't need to shout. But you could help her by using easy words.

Maria asked Liz, who lives next door, to tell her how to get to the cinema. Liz drew a simple map and told Maria to turn left out of her flat, cross two big roads, and turn left, then right, then left again. Then she had to walk about 100 metres along the main road, past some shops and restaurants, until she reached the cinema.

△ To help Maria remember her route, Liz drew a map for Maria to take with her.

Liz suggested that Maria should look out for places she would pass on the way, like the postbox on the corner, the big church and the bus station.

When you are trying to remember something, it always helps to repeat what you have been told. So, before setting off, Maria described her route to her flatmate, Tina.

◁ Tina helped Maria to check that she understood how to find the cinema.

△ Liz's map was a great help and Maria wasn't nervous about finding the cinema on her own.

With the help of Liz's map, Maria found the cinema and enjoyed the film. When she came out, it was raining, so she took the bus home. Liz had written down the name of the street where Maria would need to get off the bus. Maria showed it to the driver and he told her when they got there.

Everyone is different

Although they all have Down's syndrome, Jack, Maria, Richie and Stacey are quite different from each other. They look different, they think differently, and they are good at different things. They all have an extra chromosome but they have inherited the information on their chromosomes from different parents. So they are as different from each other as you are from the other children in your class.

▷ This baby girl will probably look like her Mum when she's older, just as her brothers look like their father.

People who have brown eyes don't all look the same, and neither do those with Down's syndrome. Richie looks much more like his father than he looks like Jack. And, when she's a little older, Stacey will not look like Maria. She will look more like her Mum.

◁ Everyone is different. Life would be very boring if we were all the same!

It's a mistake to think that people with the same problem with their health have the same abilities and disabilities. Just because two people are both blind, it doesn't mean they will be the same in other ways.

What do you do when you meet someone for the first time? You probably talk to them to find out about them. You are more likely to make friends with them if they are interested in the same things as you. Whether you have Down's syndrome or not, you will only find out what someone is like if you get to know them. You can't guess what they are like just by looking at them.

Aiming high

△ Philip Lee and his partner have to do a lot of training to get fit for their charity bike rides.

People with Down's syndrome have done some great things.

Philip Lee has ridden his bicycle in Israel and Jordan, even cycling 483 kilometres through the desert to raise money for charity.

James Van Maggs, a successful musician and dancer, has taken part in many competitions and has won awards. Despite his busy life, he has even found time to learn to speak German.

Timmy Lang is an actor and has appeared on television. He was so good at remembering his lines that the other actors called him 'One Take Tim' because they never had to film his part twice.

Tracey Young couldn't walk until she was five years old, but today she twirls around the dance floor and wins prizes for her Latin-American dancing.

△ To play the violin as well as James Van Maggs takes a great deal of practice.

△ Athletes receiving medals at the Special Olympics.

People with Down's syndrome, are among hundreds of athletes from all over the world who compete in the Special Olympics – a sports competition for people with learning and physical disabilities.

All over the world, people with Down's syndrome have been successful, whether they have got the job they wanted, appeared in a play, won prizes in sport or learned to play a musical instrument. Sometimes you have to struggle to get what you want, but if you have to work a little harder than most people, success feels even better.

If you aim high, you can do a lot with your life, whether you have learning difficulties or not. It may be tough and it may take longer than you expected, but if you want something enough, you can do it!

Making life easier

What changes would you make in the way we treat people with Down's syndrome? How could we make it easier for them to get on at school, become independent, get a job and take part in all the activities that we enjoy?

▽ Computers in schools can help people to learn different skills.

In the future, doctors may find ways to improve the eyesight and hearing of people with Down's syndrome, and to treat their heart problems more easily. Perhaps they will also be able to help children with Down's syndrome to fight off coughs, colds and other infections more effectively.

The most important thing is to give everyone the chance to learn all they can, and to use their skills. If you are good at art, like Stacey, or woodwork, like Jack, you may be able to use those skills when you are older to get a job or just to enjoy yourself and have fun.

Some people with Down's syndrome do better in ordinary schools, like the one Stacey goes to. Others prefer a special school, like Jack's. But if they don't get the chance to go to the school that suits them best, they may never do as well as they could. Parents want a wider choice of schools for children with Down's syndrome.

If people with Down's syndrome have the same opportunities as everyone else to train for a job or career they can be reliable and good at their work, like Maria. With a little help, we can all live independently. In the future, perhaps we will.

◁ Finding the right career is as important for people with Down's syndrome as it is for other adults.

Getting help

None of the medical, educational and other changes that you have just read about will make any difference to people with Down's syndrome if we don't help them too.

Everybody has felt sad or left out at some time. It isn't a very nice feeling. It is unkind and unfair to laugh, stare or ignore somebody just because they look different. Like everyone else, they feel upset and lonely when people won't give them a chance.

Children with Down's syndrome want to take part in the same activities as others of their age. They want to join clubs and groups.

◁ Groups such as the Riding For the Disabled Association help people with disabilities to enjoy horse riding.

▷ Lots of special schools, clubs and organizations arrange trips and activities especially for people with Down's syndrome.

The Down's Syndrome Association, 155 Mitcham Road, London SW17 9PG (tel. 0181 682 4001), provides help and support for people with Down's syndrome and their families. In Scotland, contact the Scottish Down's Syndrome Association, 158–160 Balgreen Road, Edinburgh EH11 3AU (tel. 0131 313 4225). Down'sED, The Sarah Duffen Centre, Belmont Street, Southsea, Portsmouth, Hampshire PO5 1NA (tel. 01705 824 261), specializes in providing educational advice and information. Mencap, Mencap National Centre, 123 Golden Lane, London EC1Y 0RT (tel. 0171 454 0454) provides help and advice for people with a learning disability.

Through these and similar organizations, people with Down's syndrome and their families can get help and advice about everyday health, education and practical problems, and they can discuss the solutions. These groups can also offer advice about training, housing and leisure activities.

Glossary

Cells The smallest parts of any living thing. The human body is made up of millions of cells, which do many different jobs.

Chromosome A thread-like structure found in cells. It carries the genes (inherited information) that play a big part in deciding how a person looks and thinks and the way their body works.

Defects Things that have gone wrong or don't work properly.

Flatmates People who share a home, even though they are not usually from the same family.

Independent Able to look after yourself without relying on other people to help or to make decisions for you.

Infections Illnesses caused by tiny organisms.

Inherit To be born with physical and mental characteristics that have been physically passed on to you by your parents.

Learning difficulties Problems learning how to do things, such as maths, reading or writing. People with learning difficulties may take longer to learn new skills.

Further information

Books

Friends at School by Rochelle Bunnet
(Starlight Books, 1995)

Our Brother has Down's Syndrome by Shelley Cairo
(Annick Press Ltd, 1991)

Big Brother Dustin by Alden R. Carter
(Albert Whitman and Co., 1997)

Veronica's First Year by Jean Sasso Rheingrove
(Albert Whitman and Co., 1996)

Thumbs up, Rico! by Maria Testa
(Albert Whitman and Co., 1994)

Websites

The Down's Syndrome Association website is:
www.downs-syndrome.org.uk

The Down'sED website is:
www.downsnet.org.uk

A list of the main sites on the Internet which are about Down's syndrome can be found at
www.davlin.net/users/lleshin

Index

Numbers in **bold** refer to pictures.